DALLAS

COWBOYS

CHIP LOVITT

CREATIVE ★ EDUCATION

Published by Creative Education
123 South Broad Street, Mankato, Minnesota 56001
Creative Education is an imprint of The Creative Company

Designed by Rita Marshall
Cover illustration by Rob Day

Photos by: Allsport Photography, Bettmann Archive, Fotosport, FPG
International, Spectra Action, and SportsChrome.

Library of Congress Cataloging-in-Publication Data

Lovitt, Chip.
Dallas Cowboys / by Chip Lovitt.
p. cm. — (NFL Today)
Summary: Traces the history of the team from its beginnings through 1996.
ISBN 0-88682-789-2

1. Dallas Cowboys (Football team)—History—Juvenile literature.
[1. Dallas Cowboys (Football team) 2 Football—History.]
I. Title. II. Series.

GV956.D3L68   1996   96-15223
796.332'64'097642812—dc20

3456

Nestled in the seemingly endless stretches of Texas prairie is the city of Dallas, which lies along the Trinity River in the northern part of the state. The second largest city in Texas, it was named, in 1846, after George Mifflin Dallas, who was then the Vice President of the United States.

Known for its mild winters and scorching summers, Dallas is the leading banking and financial hub of the Southwest, as well as a major center for publishing, advertising and manufacturing. Dallas is also in the heart of football country. Each year, the city hosts the Cotton Bowl, the annual college football classic. With powerhouse college teams such as Texas, Southern

Bob Lilly (#74) was the Cowboys' first draft choice in 1961.

Methodist, Texas Tech and Texas A & M located throughout the state, Texas football fans have lots to cheer about.

But Dallas residents are particularly proud of their pro team, the Dallas Cowboys. Since the Cowboys came to town in 1960, they have become one of the dominant teams in the National Football League (NFL), winning four Super Bowls and playing in more Super Bowls and NFC championship games than any other franchise in history.

1 9 5 2

Tex Schramm was the team president for three decades.

THE DALLAS TEXANS

The NFL first came to Texas in 1952 in the form of a team called the Dallas Texans. The Texans had high hopes and a roster of respectable talent, but unfortunately, few people were interested in watching them play. The team played to sparse crowds and won only one game. By the end of the first season, the Dallas Texans were out of business. It was the only team that ever dropped out of the NFL.

By 1959, rumors of NFL expansion began circulating. Dallas multi-millionaire Clint Murchison, Jr. was excited by the idea of bringing back pro football to his hometown, so he hired the former general manager of the Los Angeles Rams, Tex Schramm, to help put together a new team. To make sure that this new team would not be confused with the 1952 failed franchise, Schramm chose a new name—the Dallas Cowboys.

Schramm had the difficult task of assembling talent for a team that had not yet been formally admitted to the NFL and could not officially participate in the NFL Draft. Schramm's most pressing need was for a quality quarterback. His choice was the 6-foot-3, two-time All-American quarterback from Southern

Linebacker Thomas Henderson joined the Dallas defense in 1975 (page 7).

Methodist, "Dandy" Don Meredith. To sign Meredith, he asked for help from an old friend, Chicago Bears owner George Halas. Halas drafted Meredith for the Bears and then traded him to Dallas for a ninth-round draft pick in 1962. With more behind-the-scenes help, Schramm managed to sign another fine player, running back Don Perkins. On December 28, 1959, Schramm named Tom Landry head coach of the newly-formed team. One month later, the club was finally admitted to the NFL.

1 9 6 0

Don Meredith joined the Cowboys after a successful college career at Southern Methodist University.

THE COWBOYS ARE COMING TO TOWN

For the Cowboys to be competitive in their first year, Landry and Schramm decided that they needed an experienced quarterback to lead the team while Meredith got acquainted with the NFL. So they signed Eddie LeBaron, former quarterback for the Washington Redskins. Even with LeBaron, however, the Dallas offense sputtered badly and the Cowboys finished with a 0-11-1 record. It was the worst record any NFL team had chalked up since 1944.

The Cowboys started strong in 1961. After four games, they were in a four-way tie for first place in the Eastern Division with a 3-1 record. Unfortunately, the Cowboys won just one more game that season, finishing 4-9-1, but they were clearly improving.

Running back Don Perkins, whose broken foot had kept him sidelined during the 1960 season, rushed for 815 yards and was named NFL Rookie of the Year in 1961. The speedy halfback would go on to finish among the top 10 NFL rushers in each of his eight seasons and was selected six times to the Pro Bowl.

As for the Cowboys defense, it was considerably strengthened by the addition of defensive end Bob Lilly, who was the Cowboys' first draft choice ever in 1961. Lilly, a fast and strong pass rusher, was nicknamed "Mr. Cowboy" and soon developed into one of football's greatest defensive tackles. In 1979, Lilly, an 11-time Pro Bowl selection, became the first Cowboys inductee into the Pro Football Hall of Fame. "A player like Bob Lilly comes along just about once in a lifetime," Coach Tom Landry said.

Despite the talents of Perkins, Lilly and Meredith, the Cowboys continued to have losing seasons until 1965, when they finished 7-7. One reason for the turnaround was the addition of rookie wide receiver Bob Hayes. Hayes, a world champion sprinter, could outrun any defensive back and was a constant threat in long-pass situations. The Cowboys went to the playoffs for the first time in 1965, but lost to the Baltimore Colts 35-3.

Over the next four years, the Cowboys posted a combined 42-12-2 record and made the playoffs each season. They even appeared in the NFL championship game in 1966 and 1967, losing both times to the Green Bay Packers. But it was not until they added quarterback Roger Staubach to their lineup that the Cowboys really prospered—and found themselves in their first Super Bowl.

1 9 6 6

Bob Lilly and the rest of the "Doomsday Defense" exploded for over sixty quarterback sacks.

THE STAUBACH SENSATION

Roger Staubach was a Cincinnati high school football star in the late 1950s. When his first college choice, Notre Dame, failed to recruit him, he decided to give the U.S. Naval Academy a try. Staubach was the number-six quarterback in spring practices before his sophomore year, but in the fourth game of that season, he came off the bench and passed for one touchdown and ran for two more. He took over the starting spot, and the

Emmitt Smith was the Cowboys' rushing leader in the 1990s (pages 10-11).

1 9 7 5

Dallas eliminated Minnesota in the playoffs with Roger Staubach's fifty-yard "Hail Mary" pass to Drew Pearson.

next season he won college football's most prestigious honor, the Heisman Trophy.

After Staubach graduated, he was drafted by Dallas in 1964. But Staubach first had to fulfill a four-year commitment with the Navy. Even though he was stationed on ships overseas, he still practiced throwing passes. By the time he joined the Cowboys in 1969, he was still in good enough shape to win the starting quarterback job in his first pro training camp. Nicknamed "Roger the Dodger" because of his scrambling ability, Staubach led the Cowboys to an 11-2-1 record in his rookie season. In his second year, 1970, he guided the team all the way to Super Bowl V, in which they lost 16-13 to Baltimore. But Staubach and the Cowboys returned the next year to Super Bowl VI, in which they dominated the Miami Dolphins 24-3 for the Cowboys' first-ever world championship.

"My most satisfying moment as a professional was in that locker room in New Orleans," Staubach said of Super Bowl VI. "Dallas had been a winning team, but until that moment had the reputation of not being able to win the big one. I looked around that locker room at Bob Lilly, Chuck Howley and the other veterans. I could see the pride on their faces. It was a great feeling."

The 1970s turned out to be a great decade for Dallas. After that first Super Bowl championship season in 1971, the Cowboys played in five more NFC title games (1972, 1973, 1975, 1977 and 1978) and three more Super Bowls (1975, 1977 and 1978—including a 27-10 win over Denver in 1977). The Cowboys total record for the decade was the best in all the NFL, 105-39, for an exceptional winning percentage of .729

By the time Staubach retired in 1979, many sportswriters called him the best quarterback the Cowboys ever had. Known as a great clutch performer, Roger the Dodger engineered 23 come-back Cowboy victories, 14 of them in the last two minutes of the game or in overtime. He led the NFL in passing four seasons, and in 1985 he was inducted into the Pro Football Hall of Fame.

AMERICA'S TEAM

1 9 7 7

In his rookie season, running back Tony Dorsett rushed for 1,007 yards.

The Cowboys had become such an exciting and successful team that their popularity spread far beyond Texas. During the triumphant 1970s, the team was dubbed "America's Team," and the name stuck.

The pass-oriented Dallas offense grew stronger with the arrival of Tony Dorsett, the Heisman Trophy-winning running back from the University of Pittsburgh, in 1977. At 5-foot-11 and 183 pounds, Dorsett was a little man in a big man's game. However, he ran like a locomotive, barreling into his opposition with lightning speed. In his first season, Dorsett powered the Cowboys to a 12-2 season and a convincing victory over Denver 27-10 in Super Bowl XII. The next season Dorsett rushed for 1,325 yards and seven touchdowns, and the Cowboys went to the Super Bowl again, hoping to average their 21-17 loss to the Pittsburgh Steelers in Super Bowl X in 1975. But they fell again to the Steelers, 35-31.

Over the next seven years, Dorsett rushed for more than 1,000 yards each season, except for 1982, when a players' strike cut the schedule short. During those same years, Dallas made it to the NFC championship game three more times.

Dorsett holds a special place in the Cowboys' record book. He's the Cowboys' top all-time rusher with 12,036 yards and 72

Quarterback Danny White threw for 3,980 yards and 29 touchdowns—both team records.

touchdowns. His 516 career points are the second highest total in team history. And he set an NFL record for the longest run from scrimmage in football history, a 99-yard romp against the Minnesota Vikings in 1983. When Dorsett retired, he was fourth on the NFL's all-time rushing list. Only Walter Payton, Jim Brown and Franco Harris had rushed for more yardage.

Dorsett was not the only player to make a major contribution to the Cowboys in the late 1970s and 1980s. Dallas was also fortunate to have a standout quarterback take over the offense after Roger Staubach retired. Danny White began his career as a back-up quarterback, but in 1980 he got his chance to lead the Cowboys. He helped the team to a 12-4 season and the NFC championship game. White proved to be an outstanding signal-caller, and when he retired in 1988, he held team records for most touchdown passes in a career (155), a season (29) and a game (5).

In 1983, nine Dallas players with 82 combined years of NFL experience announced their retirement. The Cowboys faced the 1984 season without defensive end Harvey Martin, tight end Billy Joe DuPree, wide receiver Drew Pearson and other key veterans. That season, despite a 9-7 record, they finished next-to-last in their division. In 1986, the Cowboys finished 7-9. It was their first losing season since 1964. Although running back Herschel Walker turned in some productive performances, the Cowboys suffered through two more losing seasons in 1987 and 1988. Dallas knew they needed to make some big changes.

Herschel Walker makes a pass-grabbing leap.

On April 18, 1989, a new era in the Dallas Cowboys' history began when Arkansas-native Jerry Jones bought the team. A former college football star guard who helped the University of Arkansas win a national title in 1964, Jones was determined to turn his team around. One of his first moves was to replace Tom Landry—the only head coach the Cowboys had ever had—with Jimmy Johnson, who was head coach of the University of Miami Hurricanes. Under Johnson, the Hurricanes finished second in the nation in 1986 and 1988, and were voted the country's top college team in 1987.

Nate Newton played all 16 regular season games at left tackle.

Johnson had his work cut out for him. Dallas was in a rebuilding stage, and one of the first steps the team took was to use their number one pick in the 1989 draft to obtain UCLA quarterback Troy Aikman. Aikman had been the third-rated passer in NCAA history, and he quickly proved his worth in his rookie 1989 season. In his second game, Aikman threw for 379 yards against the Cardinals, setting an NFL rookie record. But Aikman's outstanding performances were not enough to lift the Cowboys out of the NFL basement, where they finished with a miserable 1-15 record.

In 1990, Dallas drafted a 5-foot-9, 205-pound University of Florida running back named Emmitt Smith III. Smith was the 16th player picked in the draft, as some experts considered him to be too small and too slow. Smith dispelled those doubts in 1990 when he finished fifth in rushing in the NFC and scored 11 touchdowns. Smith's statistics earned him the NFL Offensive Rookie of the Year award. Smith took satisfaction in proving his critics wrong.

"Sixteen teams passed on me," he recalled. "I was beginning to think I wouldn't go until the second round. But I hope 16 teams are kicking themselves now."

Troy Aikman was a number one draft pick.

1 9 9 1

*Tight end Jay
Novacek made his
first of many Pro
Bowl appearances.*

Those teams should be kicking themselves. In 1991, Smith led
the NFL in rushing with 1,563 yards. In 1992 and 1993, he led
the league again, becoming just the fourth man to win three straight
NFL rushing titles, matching a feat performed by Hall of Famers
Jim Brown, Earl Campbell and Steve Van Buren. People began
to compare Smith to the NFL's all-time best rushers.

"I want to do what they have done," Smith said with quiet deter-
mination. "I want to be the best who ever played."

Joining Smith as a star in the Cowboys offensive lineup was
Michael Irvin, a speedy wide receiver who caught fire in 1991,
catching 93 passes to lead the NFL with 1,523 yards. Irvin, one
of 17 children, grew up poor in Fort Lauderdale, Florida. Irvin
never lost his sense of pride, though, and he developed into a
standout athlete at the University of Miami. "I've never liked the
idea of being average," the flashy Floridian said. As things turned

out, he had nothing to worry about. From the time he joined the Cowboys, Irvin ranked consistently among the league leaders in pass receptions and yardage.

With Smith leading the ground attack, and Aikman and Irvin ruling the air, the Cowboys continued their dramatic turnaround by racking up an 11-5 record in 1991 and returning to the play-offs. Dallas downed the Chicago Bears 17-13 in the first round, then was mauled by the Detroit Lions 36-6 in the second round.

1 9 9 2

Pro Bowl defensive end Charles Haley joined the Cowboys and strengthened their pass rush.

RIDING HIGH

In 1992, the Cowboys at last regained their Super Bowl championship form. Aikman was at the peak of his game, throwing for 3,445 yards and tallying 23 touchdown passes. Smith topped his own single-season rushing best with 1,713 yards. Irvin continued burning up defensive backfields, catching 78 passes for 1,396 yards.

End Charles Haley, newly-arrived from the San Francisco 49ers, spearheaded a Dallas defense that was one of the NFL's best. A fierce competitor, Haley declared, "I hate to lose. I want to be a winner and a class winner." Haley's arrival gave the Dallas defense the spark it needed.

The Cowboys finished first in the NFC Eastern Division with a 13-3 record. In the playoffs, they grounded the Philadelphia Eagles 34-10, then met the 49ers in the NFC championship. The score stood tied 10-10 at halftime. But Aikman engineered two long second-half touchdown drives, Smith rushed for two more touchdowns and the Cowboys prevailed 30-20.

Super Bowl XXVII became the jewel in the Cowboys' come-back crown. Thirteen years after their last Super Bowl appear-

Linebacker Ken Norton led the Cowboys in tackles in 1993.

ance, the Cowboys met the Buffalo Bills in front of 98,000 fans at the Rose Bowl.

Troy Aikman, who was named Super Bowl MVP, tossed four touchdown passes, hitting Michael Irvin twice and Jay Novacek and Alvin Harper once apiece. "Troy was definitely in a zone," Emmitt Smith said. The Dallas defense was also relentless, forcing two fumbles that defensive end Jimmie Jones and linebacker Ken Norton turned into touchdowns. The Cowboys crushed the Bills 52-17. The 36-point margin was the third-largest in Super Bowl history.

Defensive end Jimmie Jones was one of the anchors of the Cowboys' fearsome defense.

In 1993, the Cowboys lineup was hobbled by injuries to Aikman, Smith, Haley and Norton, but the team still managed to compile a 12-4 record to top the NFC Eastern Division. Emmitt Smith led the league in rushing with 1,486 yards, even though he missed two games early in the season. He was also named the NFL Most Valuable Player.

The Cowboys were deep in talent, but the secret to the Cowboys' repeat success was solid team effort. "You look around here," Aikman said, "and there's no doubt we have the talent. What it comes down to is we believe in ourselves, and we believe in this football team. I know it's not going to come down to what I do. It's going to come down to what we all do."

The Cowboys put away the Green Bay Packers, 27-17, in the divisional playoffs, then faced the 49ers again for the NFC championship. Coach Jimmy Johnson wasn't merely confident. He guaranteed a Cowboys win. The players made good on their coach's guarantee. They trounced the 49ers 38-21.

The Cowboys were Super Bowl-bound once more, and again their opponent was the Bills. Buffalo led 13-6 at halftime. But early in the second half, Dallas defensive tackle Leon Lett stripped the ball from the Bills' Thurman Thomas. Cowboys safety James

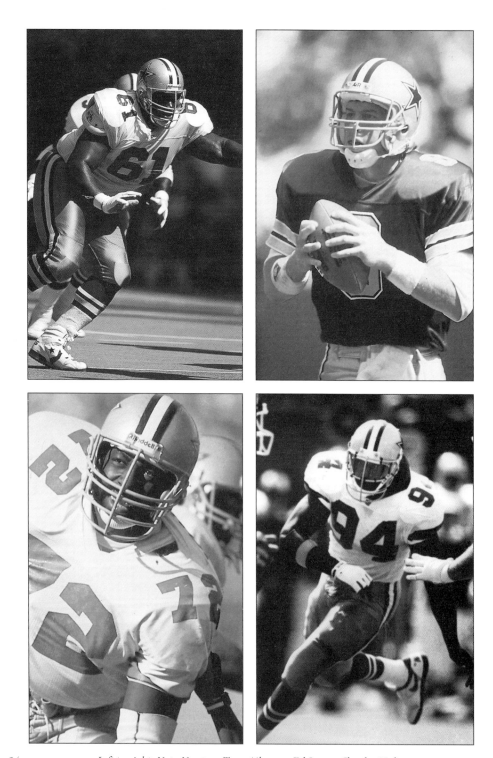

Left to right: Nate Newton, Troy Aikman, Ed Jones, Charles Haley.

Washington picked it up and raced 46 yards for the score. Powered by Emmitt Smith's 132-yard, two-touchdown performance, Dallas went on to win 30-13. It marked only the fifth time a team had won back-to-back Super Bowls.

The Cowboys got a new coach in 1994—Barry Switzer, whose University of Oklahoma teams had won three national titles. Switzer kept the Cowboys on track, taking them to a 12-4 record to top the NFC East. But the 49ers got their revenge by beating the Cowboys 38-28 in the NFC championship game.

1 9 9 5

Leon Lett made the jump to starting defensive tackle.

Dallas began the 1995 season determined to make it back to the Super Bowl once again. If the Cowboys lineup was already deep with talent, it got even deeper in October, when the team signed Deion "Prime Time" Sanders to a $35 million, seven-year contract. Sanders, a triple-threat player, could do it all—catch passes, play excellent defense, or serve on special teams.

Sanders predicted big things for himself as a Cowboy. "I expect a lot from myself. I've always wanted to be the best, and I've always wanted to create things and take them to a new level."

Sanders demonstrated what he meant in a game against the Raiders. Raiders quarterback Jeff Hostetler fired a pass to Raghib "Rocket" Ismail, who seemed to have gained a step on Sanders. Sanders turned on the speed and intercepted the pass. With his typical flashiness, Sanders taunted the Oakland players and fans by holding the ball aloft for the first ten yards of his 34-yard return. A few plays later, Emmitt Smith took the ball into touchdown territory. Sanders had promised he would make things happen and he kept his word throughout the season.

But it wasn't all a smooth ride for the Cowboys. There was tension on and off the field. Disputes flared up between the coaching staff, quarterback Troy Aikman, and several other players dur-

Michael Irvin was a favorite target of Troy Aikman (pages 26-27).

1 9 9 6

"Neon" Deion Sanders continued to be a threat both on offense and defense.

ing the season. The Cowboys also got a scare late in the season when Emmitt Smith suffered a sprained knee in a game against the Chiefs. Still, the Cowboys continued to pull together as a team when they needed to and finished with an NFL-best 12-4 record.

Once again, Emmitt Smith led the NFL in rushing with 1,773 yards and in rushing touchdowns with 25. Troy Aikman finished second in passing in the NFC. Credit for the Cowboys explosive offense also had to go to the team's massive front line. With 314-pound Erik Williams at tackles, 320-pound Nate Newton and 326-pound Derek Kennard at center, the Dallas line had the power to open holes for Smith and provide Aikman with some of the best pass protection in the game.

The Cowboys downed the Eagles in their first playoff game, then faced the Packers in the NFC championship. With the Cowboys ahead 31-27 late in the game, Brett Favre faded back and threw the ball downfield. Reading the play perfectly, defensive back Larry Wood intercepted the ball. The play set up the Cowboys' game-clinching touchdown. It also provided a preview of events soon to take place in Super Bowl XXX.

The Cowboys' Super Bowl opponent was the Pittsburgh Steelers. Dallas scored on its first three possessions to take a 13-0 lead. Just before halftime, Neil O'Donnell led the Steelers on a 54-yard touchdown drive to make the score 13-7.

In the third quarter, Dallas defensive back Larry Brown intercepted an O'Donnell pass, setting up another score that would put the Cowboys ahead 20-7. But then Pittsburgh came back and scored 10 unanswered points to narrow the Dallas lead to 20-17. Then, with just over four minutes left in the game, Pittsburgh threatened again. At his own 32-yard line, O'Donnell faded back and let go a pass. Again Larry Brown was there to intercept it. Soon thereafter, Emmitt Smith charged into the end zone to put

Troy Aikman has one of the most accurate arms in pro football.

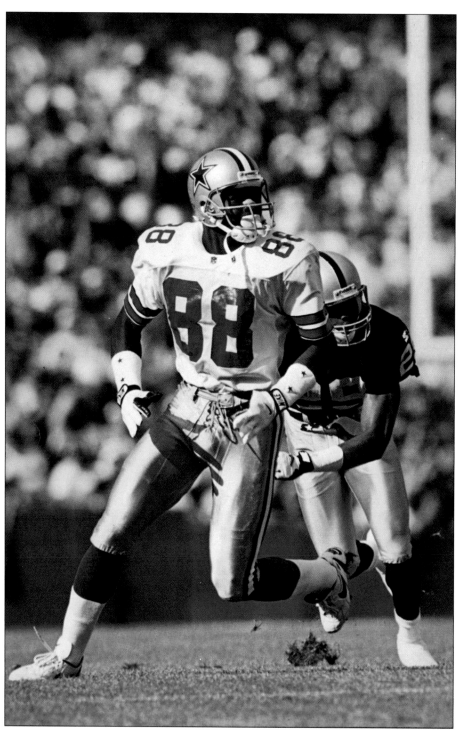

Michael Irvin, the only Dallas receiver with four Pro Bowl appearances.

Emmitt Smith, Super Bowl XXVIII MVP.

1 9 9 7

Enduring veteran Fred Strickland brings strength and speed from Green Bay.

the game on ice. The 27-17 victory was Dallas's fifth Super Bowl win, and their third in four years. For his efforts, Larry Brown was named the Super Bowl MVP.

"This is no doubt the sweetest of them all, by far," Michael Irvin said. "You can put the other two [Super Bowls] together and this one outweighs them. That's because of what we went through this year. No matter how rocky the water was at times, the bottom line was we brought the ship in."

At the post-Super Bowl press conference, Coach Switzer was asked if the Cowboys could win back-to-back Super Bowls again. "See you in New Orleans," he promised, New Orleans being the site of Super Bowl XXXI.

Whether or not the Cowboys win a record-setting sixth Super Bowl, the team's place in NFL history is already assured. And so is their status as "America's Team."